# ★ Election Day ★

### By Harriet Sigerman

Scott Foresman
is an imprint of

PEARSON

Glenview, Illinois • Boston, Massachusetts • Chandler, Arizona •
Upper Saddle River, New Jersey

All photographs are the property of Pearson Education, Inc.

ISBN 13: 978-0-328-46361-9
ISBN 10:     0-328-46361-2

1 2 3 4 5 6 7 8 9 10 V0G1 13 12 11 10 09

We are having an election.

Lily wants to be class president.

Jake does too.

Jake makes signs.

Lily makes posters.

Jake makes speeches.

Lily makes speeches too.

"Vote for me!" they say.

We vote for Jake.

Or we vote for Lily.

Who will win?

Jake gets many votes.

Lily gets more.

Lily is the new class president.

Now Lily will help our school.
Maybe Jake will help her!